# The Balloon

## Keaira Brown Jennings

4-U-Nique Publishing
*A Series of VLB/VBJ Enterprises, LLC*

4-U-Nique Publishing books may be purchased for educational, business, or sales promotional use. For information, please email: info@4-U-Nique Publishing.com

First Edition

Illustrated By: Dannii Summerfield

Cover Design By: Dannii Summerfield

Library of Congress Cataloging-in-Publication Data

ISBN-13: 978-1088182352

# The Balloon

For my daddy.
The first man I ever fell in love with.
Love you more!

"Who's in my house?"

His voice echoed as we ran to hide.

Whenever G-daddy would come home, and we were there, we would play this game. We would hide, and he would look for us. He would tickle us when he found us, and we would laugh uncontrollably. Then he would give us a big hug and ask how we were doing.

We loved going to visit our grandparents, Mimi and G-daddy. They always spoiled us.

Mimi got a puppy for herself, but she always said it belonged to all of us, but I thought it was only my puppy! G-daddy always had boxes of Mike N Ike candy in the house waiting for us. He would sneak us candy when he thought Mommy was not looking, but she always saw.

Their home was always filled with lots of love and laughs.

We had lots of fun doing things with Mimi and G-daddy. We would go to the pool, play games, go to museums, and go to the movies. One time during Christmas, my whole family even went to visit the White House in Washington, D.C. That was so exciting!

DAY OUT TO
THE MUSEUM

SWIMMING

CHRISTMAS AT THE
WHITE HOUSE

GAME NIGHT!

MOVIES

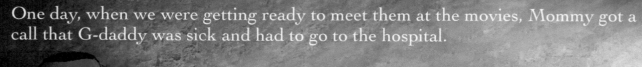

One day, when we were getting ready to meet them at the movies, Mommy got a call that G-daddy was sick and had to go to the hospital.

That was the day
that **everything changed.**

We went to visit G-daddy in the hospital. He was laughing and talking to us. That made us feel much better.

He was there for just a few days. We were so happy when he was finally able to come home.

When G-daddy came home, things were never the same. We never got to play "Who's in My House" because he was always tired. Even though he could not run and play like he used to, he still asked us about school and what we had been up to. He always told us to make sure we were reading lots of books and to sit up straight!

After a few months, G-daddy had to go back to the hospital. This time, we could not visit him. When we would go to the hospital, we always had to stay in the waiting room or cafeteria with a grown-up.

We just wanted to see G-daddy, but no one would let us, and we hated that.

We were so sad and scared.

One weekend, Daddy told us we were going to take a ride to the country to visit his parents, our other grandparents, Mama and Papa.

We always had fun down there.

Mommy did not go with us because she wanted to stay home so she could be with G-daddy in the hospital.

It was a 4-hour drive, so we went to sleep on the ride while Daddy drove. It was nighttime when we finally arrived at Mama and Papa's. When the car stopped, I woke up and could see that it was dark, but the sky was so clear, and we could see all the stars.

There was one star right above us that was so bright. It was amazing! The star kept blinking. It looked like it was trying to get our attention to say hi. With tears in his eyes, Daddy said, "Look, do you guys see that star? That is G-daddy coming to tell you he loves you."

"What do you mean, Daddy?" We all asked.

It was at that moment that everything we knew changed forever. Daddy said Mommy called while we were on our drive and told him that G-daddy went to live in heaven.

I cried so hard that I made myself sick. My brothers tried to be strong, but they were crying too. I even saw my Daddy cry.

We called Mommy and told her we were coming back home. After Daddy rested for a bit, we got back in his truck, and we went home. It seemed like it took forever to get there.

Everyone was sad, and no one was talking.

I felt a pain in my chest.
It was my heart hurting.

That was the worst day ever!'

When we finally got to Mimi and G-daddy's house, I ran into the kitchen and gave Mimi a big hug. She was so sad.

Then I ran to my Mommy, hugging her and crying. She held me tight. Her hugs always made me feel better, but it did not help that day.

My brothers went into the living room. One was lying on the couch crying, and the other looked like he wanted to cry but could not because he was in shock.

We were all so sad.

I asked Mommy what happened and why G-daddy had to go to heaven. She sat down with my brothers, put me on her lap, and took a deep breath.

"Well," she said slowly, "G-daddy was sick, so he needed to go to heaven so he would not be sick anymore."

"But I miss him! How come he had to go?" I said through my cries.

"Well, Shug" that is Mommy's nickname for me. "His body was sick, sweetie, so his spirit had to leave his body and go back to heaven." I did not understand what she meant.

"You know how you love to play with balloons?" Mommy asked me.

I shook my head yes as I wiped my tears.

"When you get your balloons, they are flat, and you cannot play with them. You can only play with them when you fill them up with air. Once you fill them with air, they come to life. You can toss them up and play games with them. But over time, the balloon gets old, and the air inside slowly leaves the balloon. The air that used to be in the balloon is now all around you. You cannot see it, but you can feel it, so you know it is there."

My brothers and I sat looking at Mommy as she continued to talk.

"This is what happens to us. We cannot do anything when God creates us until He fills us with His air. That air is our spirit. He breathes life into our bodies, and when our bodies get too old or too sick, our spirits leave our bodies, just like the air in the balloon. And just like the air in the balloon, you cannot see the spirit, but it is still there. Even though you cannot see G-daddy, he is still around."

Mommy gave us a big hug, and we just sat there in her arms for a while.

This time, her hug made me feel better.

After a few days, our family and friends came to honor G-daddy. There were so many people. I never knew G-daddy knew so many people. His favorite color was royal blue so everyone wore that color. It was so pretty.

We sang songs, cried, laughed, and talked about all the funny things G-daddy used to do and say. It made me happy to think of the fun games he would play with me, my brothers, and my cousin.

I was still sad because I missed him. Mommy and Daddy said I would always miss him, but he would always be around, just like the air in the balloon.

Mimi told me I would know when he was around. "How will I know he is around if I can't see him?" I asked. She said, "Your heart will tell you he is near. Don't worry."

One day, when I was in my room and feeling sad because I missed G-daddy so much, I saw a white feather on my dresser. I noticed that every time I was sad, I would find a white feather. Mommy and Mimi said G-daddy was letting me know he was around. I asked Mommy if I could put pictures of me and G-daddy in my room so I could see him whenever I wanted. Mommy printed pictures for me, and she took me to pick out a pretty glass jar to keep the feathers from G-daddy in. I keep the jar on my dresser, and every time G-daddy comes and leaves me a feather, I put it in my jar as a reminder that he is always around…

...Just like the air in
**the balloon.**

All sales from this book will be donated to Love U More Foundation, Inc.

Love U More Foundation, Inc. seeks to carry out the legacy of the life of Ronald E. Brown (G-daddy) as he left us with an incredible legacy of one man's heart for Christ. Not many knew of the many acts of kindness and charitable contributions that he provided as it was not his way to boast or brag, but rather live by the tenant in Matthew 7:16. Whenever someone would tell him "I love you" his response was always "I love you more!"

Love U More Foundation was established to address the needs of at-risk children and their families. Every child deserves to feel the sense of security that comes from knowing their food, clothing, shelter, and educational needs will never be in jeopardy, so they can focus on enjoying their childhood. Love U More Foundation also seeks to cultivate new opportunities for children, their families, and the communities which they reside in, through the use of literacy, technology, and exposure to things that they would not otherwise have access to.

To learn more about Love U More Foundation please visit www.loveumore.org

# About the Author

Keaira Brown Jennings embodies the spirit of a servant leader, a devoted mother, a compassionate friend, and an unwavering advocate for the joy and well-being of every child.

The divine inspiration behind this extraordinary story comes from Keaira's cherished role as a loving daughter. Within the intimate moments shared with her family, she discovers the profound magic of connection, imagination, and the power of a tender heart. Brown Jennings believes in the transformative power of storytelling and uses her gift to ignite the sparks of wonder and curiosity in young readers' minds.

Keaira Brown Jennings has dedicated herself to philanthropic endeavors that uplift and empower children from all walks of life. Her unwavering commitment to creating a better world for the next generation shines brightly, illuminating the path for others to follow.

Printed in the USA
CPSIA information can be obtained
at www.ICGtesting.com
LVHW071532240823
756146LV00007B/194